See the Lleyn Peninsula

by

Tony Roberts

Illustrations:
Elizabeth Roberts

Lleyn Sheep

First Impression 1992

Published by
E. A. Roberts, Abercastle Publications
Haverfordwest, Pembrokeshire, Dyfed

Printed by
Dinefwr Press, Llandybïe, Dyfed

Contents

Preface

This is a short and rather impressionistic guide-book, basically for people visiting the area. Lleyn is a beautiful and unspoilt place, quiet and gentle: a background, we have felt, in which old medieval churches *et hoc genus* may legitimately be seen to greatest advantage and emphasized. As a counter-weight, we have therefore devoted some pages suggesting other things to be seen, including some beyond the immediate area.

Ty'n Pwll, Rhoshirwaun, 1900

Seeing Lleyn

There is a great paucity of guide books on the Lleyn peninsula. In fact there are not many about Wales that go into any local detail. There have been some very good ones, but nowadays they seem to go out of print after a few years and what one had always regarded as the standard guide books just do not seem to be available. And the Lleyn peninsula is certainly worth more than the odd couple of pages in a country-wide guide. So, no apologies for this small new guide devoted entirely to the area. One has to assume that the normal means of transport is by car: it can't be by rail, or one wouldn't get past Pwllheli and the bus services are too rudimentary for frequent stops and re-starts.

So, we drive round the perimeter from Caernarvon to Aberdaron and then eastwards to Pwllheli and on to Porthmadog. Then, to complete the triangle, by going north up the A487 to Caernarvon. But, most important, we shall go as much as possible through the small roads that connect the little villages of the interior, if one can use such a term when you are rarely more than a few miles from the coast. Nonetheless, there is plenty of scope for getting lost, but rarely for long. The sea view is ever present though it is debatable if it offers any better views than those from the rare hills. Indeed, it is quite possible to argue that nowhere in Wales, which means in the whole of Britain, gives more satisfyingly spectacular views of hill, lowland and sea.

But there is more to Lleyn than that. Although the peninsula is rather out on a limb, well before recorded history it played a key role in the life of Wales. Together with Anglesey, it is supreme in the north in providing records of the prehistoric life of the country; and throughout recorded history it has been a bastion of Welsh culture and language, which even the recent influx of incomers has not removed. The word Lleyn is related to Leinster and the early historical connexion with Ireland has been strong.

The eastern limit we have chosen is not in fact part of the Lleyn peninsula – where the peninsula starts is open to question.

What is there to see and How to see it

Lleyn is the most remote and unspoiled part of Wales and there are not many trunk roads, thank goodness. It is also widely regarded as the most Welsh part of Wales, both in language and culture; it still has the highest proportion of Welsh speakers of any part. But like other areas, it is poor and there is an export of young people, and as elsewhere an import of English, especially second-homers and retired. And since no London government cares what happens to rural life, it is in a state of decline.

It is also an official Area of Outstanding Natural Beauty, or parts of it at least, one of those strange categories like National Park, which serve to enhance property values but prevent economic development on aesthetic grounds. So, we can expect a pretty near subsistence agriculture, little or no industry, some council homes, though not recently, and some marinas and a number of new houses, invariably unsuited to the landscape.

What it boils down to is that one can expect a superb rural landscape of hills and valleys, some wooded; there are scarcely any towns, and the villages are small too. It has to be a looking backward landscape, but within those limits, it hardly can be bettered. Once beneath the holiday superficiality, is a historical reality that encapsulates Wales. And to get full value from what is there, one must look a little beneath the surface and delve a bit into the prehistory and the early medieval history of the country.

And if the pleasures we indicate seem a little too esoteric, it is no great distance to go over eastward into Snowdonia and to Anglesey or Merioneth or on to the north coast to Llandudno, Rhyl and Colwyn Bay.

First, Lleyn itself. As you can see from the sketch map, there is a triangle of roads that bounds the area we have called the Lleyn peninsula. Some people reckon that Lleyn proper extends only westward of a line roughly joining Pwllheli and Nefyn, but this is to be unnecessarily legalistic, depending on medieval boundaries.

The name Lleyn has associations with Ireland and indeed there were many early local contacts as with Pembrokeshire, the other projecting part of Wales, both in prehistoric and medieval times.

Let us start on the Caernarvon-Porthmadog road (A487); leave at Bryncir, turn right to Cennin. Mynydd Cennin lies ahead. Go either rightabout or leftabout round it and carry on towards Llangybi, our first stop. You are plunged straight into the rural heart of the peninsula. There are lots of little roads many with no sign posts.

There is nothing special about this bit of countryside, except that it is one of the pleasantest you can find. This area in the middle of the penin-

St. Cybi's Well

sula is called the Pant Glas – Ynys Depression, and it is dismissed in the text-books as poorish agricultural land of heather, bracken and gorse. It is boulder clay and drift which breaks up the patches of marshy flats with big cones of igneous rock standing up like little mountains.

It is too poor land for more than rough grazing for beef cattle and sheep. Little scattered farms, tiny hamlets and an almost complete absence of modernisation. While the northern coastline and much of the south has been designated an Area of Outstanding Natural Beauty, this particularly attractive part is not. Just as well: the usual visible evidence for such designations is wider roads, bigger car parks and imposing public lavatories.

So, onto Llangybi, a cluster of houses with a church; the latter has a late 15th century chancel; porch, bell-cote, etc. were added in a late Victorian restoration. But what you must not miss here is St. Cybi's well. Despite its modestly rural setting, this is a famous site. St. Cybi traditionally came from Cornwall in the 6th century, establishing a cell on the Pembrokeshire coast and a monastery at Holyhead. There are quite elaborate buildings here, all ruined now, and in any case later than St.

Cybi. There was a cottage, bath-house and bath built in 1750 by Mr William Price of Rhiwlas.

Water from the well used to be carried away in bottles for use as medicine and it was claimed to be a cure for warts, lameness, blindness, scurvy and rheumatism. It was also used to divine a lover's intentions and an eel living in it was thought to give much virtue.

This may well have been one of the pagan wells converted to Christianity, as the Church instructed. Or it may be that Cybi just wanted to be able have a drink of water near an early cell, but the curative properties would seem to favour the former. At any rate, this pastoral setting gives one the impression of plunging back into medieval times almost at one fell swoop. Right behind the well, rearing to the north is Garn Pentyrch on the top of which is an Iron Age fortlet.

So, on to Y Ffor, or Four Crosses, where the B4354 cuts across the A499 north to south road. If you want to linger, bear in mind that there is a fine Neolithic burial chamber; at least four standing stones within a couple of miles radius. So, if all seems quiet nowadays, there was at least as much activity between a thousand back to four thousand years ago. But if you do not feel anything about the continuity of history, Butlins Camp and the beaches are only a couple of miles to the south on the coast.

But before moving on, one other thing: just up the road past Pencaenewydd is Lake Glasfryn. This was said to have owed its origin to the overflowing of the Ffynnon Grasi, the nearby well, whose stone cover had been left off through an oversight by a lady named Grasi (Grace?) who then haunted the field, and the house close by; and was changed into the standing stone looking like a woman in the field Cae'r Ladi, 'the Lady's Field'. The land is private.

Still on the A499, on the road towards Llanaelhaearn is the 'Welsh Lady' factory, making good jams, marmalades; you will probably see them in local shops.

There is no straight road down the peninsula to Aberdaron; you have to zig-zag a bit; though you can go in any direction you like and check up the interesting things in the index. From Y Ffor you can just as easily go north to Llanaelhaearn, west to Nefyn, south to Pwllheli; but we'll go to Aberdaron anyway – all roads lead to Aberdaron in the end.

There is quite a lot written about the Pilgrim's Road to Aberdaron, or rather to Bardsey, but in fact there is no such track traceable, though certain of the churches are known to have been pilgrims' churches. But if you wish to wander south-westwards, the road is not entirely straightforward, and there are no towns and few villages.

The B4354 goes dead straight towards Nefyn. It was intended to be the

Capel Newydd, Nanhoron, 1770

route of a railway when Dinas Dinlle was to be the terminus for the route to Dublin, of which more later.

Just before the junction of the B4354 and the A497 is Garn Boduan with an Iron Age fort on top. Actually in two parts, a large one with a fortification enclosing over 170 hut circles and a small summit fort that may well have Buan's own residence. Buan, Bodfuan, Bodvean are variations of the same name.

Boduan village is tiny, the Hall is now an hotel. It was the seat of the Winn (Newborough) family, in early 18th century, with Victorian additions, and fine beech and rhododendrons in the woods. Church is late Victorian dedicated to St. (courtesy title, as are pretty well all of the Saints) Buan who possibly set up his shrine in the late 6th century.

Weave your way southwards, turn right at Efail Newydd to Rhyd-y-Clafdy on the B4415. You pass Bodfel Hall, which could be well worth a stop. Historically, the place where Mrs Thrale, friend of Dr. Johnson, was born. Her rather unWelsh name, Salusbury, is that of a family with several hundred years history in north Wales, mostly further east in Clwyd. Nowadays a country pursuits and crafts centre, coffee shop too.

Take the A4415 south-west down the lovely wooded Nanhoron valley, then to Botwnnog and on to Sarn Mellteyrn and the B4413 to Aberdaron.

Bottwnnog is a very small village with a little 19th century rebuilt church, dedicated to St. Beuno, some of the woodwork of which was rescued from an Italian ship wrecked off Porth Neigwl.

Sarn Mellteyrn has potters and three pubs as well as a Victorian church, well sited overlooking the valley. Pleasant and nicely situated village. A slightly unusual claim to fame is that the South African poet Roy Campbell lived here for a while, perhaps best remembered for his comments on certain poets:

> "You praise the restraint with which they write,
> I'm with you there of course
> I see the snaffle and the curb all right
> But where's the bloody horse?"

Mellteyrn close by has a different claim: birthplace of Henry Rowlands, Bishop of Bangor, who built one of the earliest Grammar Schools in Wales at Bottwnnog a few miles away. Below Carn Fadryn in a wooded situation, is Llaniestyn, a couple miles north-east, a remarkably attractive church. Double nave, as so often occurs in north Wales; and with an unusual musicians' gallery, fine late medieval font. Llandudwen is a village which you might well miss if you go along the coast road. It is on the north slopes of Garn Fadryn, very tiny but an interesting church. The church itself is isolated in farmland. Dedicated to Saint Tudwen, relative of St. David. Founded in 5th century, but present building is medieval. Rare pre-Reformation silver chalice and 10th century octagonal font. One does rather concentrate on the churches in the these villages, but there are precious few secular buildings to emphasise. Good example here. Madryn Castle nearby is far from being the original house, but the ruined gatehouse is a fine Tudor relic.

Garn Fadryn is the most impressive Iron Age hill fort south of Yr Eifl. A 12-acre site was protected by a stone wall and this was doubled by a similar defence taking in the upper slopes. A most interesting north and south gateway and zig-zagged terraced roadways put in at a later phase. Only about ten houses inside the enclosure but nearly a hundred on the slopes. Probably pre-Roman round houses, and the larger number of irregular enclosures post or late Roman times. The small fort on the summit has a dry-stone wall round. Giraldus Cambrensis recorded a newly-built stone castle when he was on his Crusade enlistment campaign in 1188. The top fort is traditionally 'the castle of the Sons of Owain'.

Fifteen people to the acre has been estimated as the probable population in these north Wales forts: Tre'r Ceiri, Boduan, Fadryn, so there was quite likely a pretty high population density hereabouts fifteen hundred or two thousand years ago.

Continuing along the B4413, the next point of interest, in fact the only one before Aberdaron, is also archaeological. This is Castell Odo, quite easy to overlook. It is a low hill on the right-hand side about a mile and a half before Aberdaron. This was the first Iron Age fort to be excavated in Lleyn. There were actually five different phases of occupation, starting as far back as the 4th century B.C. And this may well have been the earliest

Mellteyrn Church

settlement of the Celts in north Wales. Certainly some of the pottery found there suggests that it may.

It is not a very commanding site to defend; more like what are now being called defended settlements but it is in a commanding position above the beach at Aberdaron and the little river valleys which converge there: a likely place for early settlers coming by sea.

Thence down to Aberdaron, the Land's End of Wales. But before going down the hill into the village, one should go over towards Braich y Pwll, the headland. This, so much more impressive than the Cornish Land's End, is a headland of heather and gorse, grazed by sheep. Wonderful views seaward and to Bardsey Island southwards from the coastguard look-out post. National Trust property, splendid walking. Beneath Mynydd Mawr is Ffynnon Ffair (St. Mary's Well) with a footpath down. The well may be covered by the sea at high water but the well water stays pure. Remains of an ancient church down on the shore. Take a cupful of water from the well, the legend says, go up and walk three times round the well without spilling a drop, and your wish will be granted.

Aberdaron is a pleasant little village, once called remote. The railway stopped at Pwllheli and there isn't one on the north coast, but with motor transport, Aberdaron has become simply the furthest point on Lleyn, and 'rediscovered' as the Shell Guide has it. Busy and popular in summer but scarcely bigger, so residents, summer visitors and second-homers are all crowded in the steep narrow streets, over the medieval hump-backed bridge and on the beach, which is a good sandy one though exposed to the south-west.

Historically though, there is much more to it than a holiday resort. It was from the 6th century, the final stop for pilgrims wanting to get to Bardsey Island. Y Gegin Fawr, now a restaurant, in the middle of the village was a medieval rest-house and eating place. The church, St. Hywyn's, was found in the 6th century though the present building is some six hundred years later or thereabouts – the doorway at least is Norman. It became a clas church, which made it very important in early Celtic Christianity, Clynnog Fawr being the only other one on Lleyn.

Clas churches were 'community' churches for a number of holy men, unlike the tiny ones built by or for single monks.

It became a medieval place of sanctuary; in the 12th century, Gryffydd ap Rhys, Prince of South Wales, was going to be handed over to the rather brutal Henry I by Gruffydd ap Cynan, Prince of the North. Anyway, the united clergy had enough moral (and possibly physical) force to prevent it. Cromwell reputedly stabled his horses in it. In Victorian times, they thought a new sea-wall would cost more than a new church, so they started building the latter. There was an outcry, and it was decided that the sea-wall could be shored up, and St. Hywyn's stayed. The Post Office was designed by the builder of Portmeirion, Sir Clough Williams-Ellis (there is a nice little leaflet on a Williams-Ellis tour – ask at an Information Centre).

A famous agreement was signed here at Aberdaron. The Tripartite Indenture of 1405 was to divide up Britain: Wales would become independent again, under Glyndŵr; The Percies of Northumberland would take the North and Midlands, and Mortimer the South. Sadly, they reckoned without Henry IV and his son later, Henry V. Holinshed got it wrong and said they signed in Bangor, and Shakespear followed him.

Bardsey holds a special place in Welsh history, more than any other island, and its name is held in a similar respect as St. David's itself. The Welsh name for Bardsey, Ynys Enlli, means Island of the Current and the

Y Gegin Fawr, Aberdaron

wind, tides and currents make the crossing difficult and at times precarious.

The first recorded settlement is that of the survivors of the massacre by the Saxons of the monks of Bangor Is-coed; but it could have been a settlement by St. Cadfan a little earlier. St. Dyfrig (Dubricius) retired and died here, and legend has it that twenty thousand saints lie buried. The island has a special holiness and it relates to the old Celtic Church rather than to that of Augustine. Three pilgrimages were equal to one to Jerusalem. This is the end point of the pilgrimage made through the ages and gives a poignancy to the small churches linked along the north coast of Lleyn. It is a sense of place and history rather than of actual buildings; none of the earliest remains. And nothing of Merlin, reputedly here with the 13 Treasures of Britain in his house of glass.

On his tour through Wales, Giraldus did not come nearer here than Nefyn but he recorded that nobody died except in order of seniority, oldest first, on account of the good climate.

A monastery was started in the 12th century, minimal remains though. Since the Middle Ages, the island has belonged to the Wynns of Newborough but it is now owned by a Trust and it is an important ornithological Observatory. Of minor historical interest now is the curious

Y Mownt Aberdaron

From Yr Eifl towards Nefyn

institution of the 'King', one of the tenants chosen to 'govern' the community. This was instituted by Lord Newborough but lapsed with the passing of a genuine farming community. Now one couple only farms here, but there is accommodation for bird watchers. The institution is paralleled nowadays by the Captain of the beach at Aberdaron, appointed to keep it ship-shape.

The lighthouse, built in 1821 by Nelson, 'a handsome square structure', attracted so many of the migrant birds that a decoy was put up. Among the important residents are the choughs, who have been much studied, and the Manx shearwaters. The 500ft. mountain is in the north of the island, an anchorage in the middle and grassy turf in the south.

Now we shall go along the north coast

When you leave Caernarvon, the main roads take you through and round Snowdonia or to Bangor. The A487 is the one which we have rather arbitrarily taken as the eastern limit of Lleyn. But to 'do' the north coast of the peninsula, break off as soon as possible taking the right-hand fork to stay as near the sea as you can. It is not very exciting country round Foryd Bay and you could well be pardoned for missing it and going on down the main coast road A499. If you do, go only as far as Llanaelhaearn because the main road goes to Pwllheli. But Foryd Bay is interesting for a couple of things. Firstly, it is good bird-watching country, and secondly, Llanfaglan Church is worth seeing.

The church stands alone, a bit desolate, surrounded by trees, churchyard and open country. The 19th century restoration movement missed it. A Roman stone memorial inscribed to Anetemor, son of Lovernius, has been utilised as a doorway lintel. This whole area – we are not far from Segontium – was occupied by the Romans, and there are other Roman stones used in walls. A bit further on to the south is a car park, useful for bird-watching over Foryd Bay.

Things worth seeing either side of the main road: on the seaward side first is Dinas Dinlle. A mile below the village is an eroded hill surrounded by two massive banks, an Iron Age beach-head fortification, 2nd and 3rd century AD finds. It may be that the Romans built inside the banks and perhaps a causeway to Segontium (Caernarvon). There are modern holiday developments, a sandy beach and a straight road to Caernarvon Airfield where there is a museum and pleasure flights.

Fort Belan was built here in the late 18th century together with Fort Williamsburg, which rather surprisingly is in Glynllifon Park. Thomas Wynn, first Lord Newborough, built both, playing around, as many landowners did, with his own militia as an anti-French defence.

This leads one to Glynllifon Park, on the other side of the A499. Llandwrog village was a Victorian estate village built by Lord Newborough, with its trim little 1860s church which has Wynn monuments. More like Port Sunlight than the Lleyn, though Glynllifon has more to do with anglicised patronage than Welshness.

Glynllifon is behind the walls on the main road. Owned by the local authority now, it is a bit of curate's egg of a place. The house is a college and not open, but there are craft workshops and a wildlife park: well worth a visit. The other 18th century fort, Williamsburg, was built in the park as was a Mausoleum but this was never finished.

Back on to the A499, going south

Out to sea is Caer Arianrhod. Together with Dinas Dinlle, this brings us into the realm of the early folk-tale. It relates to one of the main tales in the Mabinogion. This is a famous collection of Welsh folk-tales written in late medieval times, but probably existing for many hundreds of years as oral tales. In Math, son of Mathonwy, the hero Lleu was the son of the virgin Arianrhod. His father (uncle?) hid him, perhaps at Dinas Dinlle. Caer Arianrhod (Arianrhod's Castle) may have been her citadel. But, this is a romantic 16th century invention; there is a submerged reef, not a ruined building.

Before coming to Clynnog Fawr, it is pleasant to turn off the main road and explore the countryside on the left; narrow roads, picturesque if not fertile fields; turn at Pontllyfni, whose beach is hardly the finest, and up to Pont-y-Cim, where there is a fine little early 17th century bridge. Further on is Felin Faesog, a little Museum of Welsh Country Life in an old flour mill.

Clynnog Fawr is well-known principally because of its magnificent church. The great periods of church building in England by-passed Wales; but not here.

The village is quite small and agreeable, and the massive church is on the site of the original cell of St. Beuno, most important of north Wales holy men. It was a *clas* or community church, later called collegiate. Aberdaron was the other clas church in Lleyn.

Immediately one is struck by the magnificent windows, then the battlements and pinnacles. Inside it is big by any standards, huge by Welsh, and unfussy, light and spacious. St. Beuno's original burial place, and saint's shrine, is the sixteenth century chapel with connecting passage, on the site, it is thought, of the original cell.

The church is on the pilgrim trail to Bardsey, the most important station, and pilgrim offerings provided the money for such a building.

There are Tudor stalls with misericords in the chancel, a fine old dog tongs, and the 'Chest of Beuno' a formidable box made of one log, in which pilgrims' offerings were stored. Calves and lambs born with a natural slit in the ear were sold for St. Beuno's benefit.

As late as the 18th century, Beuno's tomb, in the middle of the chapel, was thought to have curative properties.

A holy well, about 200 yards south-west of the church, was one of the the best known curing wells in Lleyn. The cure for fits and epilepsy seems to have been linked with exposure of the patient in St. Beuno's chapel and a cure for eye troubles was made out of scrapings of stone from the columns of Beuno's chapel.

A small, good cromlech (Neolithic burial chamber) lies near the sea a few hundred yards away (go down the road past the church). Not very large but it has three uprights and a number of cupmarks cut in the top of the capstone. Cupmarks are rare in Wales and somewhat later than the Neolithic, suggesting that the turf covering had been removed as early as the Bronze Age.

On down to Llanaelhaearn; the splendid, wild, hilly landscape to the left is Bwlch Mawr, Gyrn Goch and Gyrn Ddu. You can take a circular tour from Clynnog Fawr up round Bwlch Mawr back to Llanaelhaearn. Turn off to the right before Llanaelhaearn and go down to Trefor. The granite from here provided just about the only industry in Lleyn. But it has gone now. The village has been cleaned up and is trying to look like a holiday village instead of a working one. It has cleaned up all right, though it looks as though it is waiting for something, and is not really doing anything any more.

Clynnog Fawr church, on the left, St. Beuno's Chapel

The granite mountainside quarried away was the northernmost fork of Yr Eifl, the triple peaks forming The Rivals, as Yr Eifl has been anglicised to. Mynydd Carnguwch, the other side of the road, is not regarded as one of Yr Eifl. Standing by itself on the southern slope of Mynydd Carnguwch is an isolated church, reachable on foot. Worth seeing if only as an instance of the past. The bellcote is strong and the windows square. It is marked on the O.S. map but not named.

Llanaelhaearn is pleasant but it seems to be in awe of the impressive hills around. Late Victorian restoration of medieval church, transepts 16th and 17th century, chancel Victorian. Fine box pews. St. Aelhaearn's well has become the village's water supply.

North transept has a 5th century Latin inscribed stone 'Aliortus the Elmetian lies hear'. One wonders how a man from the Saxon kingdom of Elmet in Yorkshire came to be here.

The group of hills to the north-east of Llanaelhaearn, Gyrn Goch, Bwlch Mawr, Moel and Gyrn Ddu, have a good number of hut groups, shown on the 1¼" O.S. map. All probably late Iron Age, about Roman times. Little road east of Llanaelhaearn and the footpath will take you through but it is a walk of several miles, as the road peters out.

Lithfaen is the village that leads to Yr Eifl and it is worth visiting for the views. Signpost marks the track up to Tre'r Ceiri, Town of the Giants, which crowns the top part of the landward mountain. Half an hour takes you to the top and the views are as good as anything in Wales, and on a clear day, better. This is the most important Iron Age fortress in Wales.

The outer rampart is better preserved on the north and west where it is twelve feet or more high. On the south-west, where the path leads, it is more eroded. There were some 150 huts within the walls and a large cairn right at the top, presumably Bronze Age. The highest peak has a couple of cairns but no hut circles, and the outermost cairn has hut circles and a settlement. Excavations have been done here.

Just as interesting in its way is Porth y Nant. It is no longer deserted as it used to be. Once a quarry village it was abandoned in the fifties. Now the two terraces of cottages and other village buildings have taken on new life as the Nant Gwrtheyrn Welsh Language Centre where live-in language courses are held. The valley is also called Nant Gwrtheyrn, after the early British ruler. This is intriguing; Gwrtheyrn or Vortigern has had a bad press: he is traditionally seen as the King who introduced Horsa and Hengist to Britain to help fight the Picts and Irish invaders and then they woudn't go and gradually took over the country. There was a cairn here called the Grave of Gwrtheyrn. Despite older guide books, the village is accessible by private road.

Looking towards Yr Eifl

Pistyll, next village down the main road, is on the Saints' Road to Bardsey. The church is austere and simple, single celled and dating probably from the 12th to 15th century. At Easter, Harvest and Christmas, herbs, wild plants and evergreens are strewn on the floor. The church is dedicated to St. Beuno.

A couple of miles further is Nefyn.

Rather more than a village, its air of being a small seaside resort is belied by its long history as a medieval borough with a charter dating back to 1355. It was granted by Edward the Black Prince to Nigel de Loring, and he gave him Pwllheli as well.

Perhaps its main claim to fame was the great tournament and celebrations held by Edward I after the conquest of north Wales.

But fishing – the town arms are three herrings – and coast wise shipping have long given way to tourism as the main livelihood.

Just down the road is Morfa Nefyn, rather bungaloid, overlooking Caernarvon Bay and the fine beaches Porth Nefyn and Porth Dinllaen, in the shelter of steep cliffs. Right down on the beach is the hamlet of Porth Dinllaen.

Morfa Nefyn is separated from Porth Dinllaen by the headland Penrhyn Nefyn and the hamlet of Porth Dinllaen has no road access. At low water it is possible to drive over the sands; residents get a key to drive across the golf club access.

The long narrow peninsula at Porth Dinllaen has long been a minor harbour and because it is well sheltered from the south-west, it was a firm contender for being the western terminus for the Irish traffic. In the end it lost out to Holyhead, but the straight road from Pwllheli to Nefyn

Porth Dinllaen

was where the rail extension would have come. Splendid coast walking for miles.

The road B4417 goes on past Nefyn and then turns into the B4413 down to Aberdaron. At Tudweiliog it no longer goes along the coast. From then on, there is a network of narrow roads going nowhere more or less, but giving access to, or at least letting you get near, some very pleasant beaches.

Tudweiliog is a pleasant hamlet, hardly hill-top as some guides would have it. The peninsula has narrowed by here and the road inland towards Llaniestyn goes through attractive nondescript country past Garn Fadryn to the Nanhoron valley.

Tudweiliog, like Edern, the village just by Nefyn, has a simple Victorian church. There are several good beaches close by, but first, Penllech just off the B4417, has a simple unassuming church, with early painted furniture, and at Mynydd Cefn Amlwch is a Neolithic burial chamber with three uprights. A legend says it was removed once, but the cattle complained so much it was replaced.

Porth Towyn is close to Tudweiliog. As with many beaches, parking is tricky, but there is a limited amount on the road, and a farm car-park. A small headland separates it from Porth Ysgaden (herring) which as the name suggests was once a herring harbour. Ruined buildings are still there. A bit of crab and lobster fishing still. The coast around here is pretty wild, and very pleasant. Footpaths and Porth Ysglaig separate Porth Towyn and Porth Ysgaden. Good bass fishing.

Porth Ychen is a small cove, picturesque and rocky with a shingle beach. Reached by footpath across gorse and heather covered rough some half mile off the road.

Traeth Penllech is a good length of sand best reached from Porth Colmon, a rocky harbour where you can park. Sand too. It is at the end of Traeth Penllech to which you can walk. Alternatively there is a footpath by a stream half way along, and there is a car park there. A biggish beach by the standards of this coastline.

A number of little coves, Tŷ Mawr, Widlin, etc., some accessible by footpath from the coast road; but for walking rather than beach access till Porth Iago which is sandy between rocky headlands. It faces south-west; turn off the road, pay to park at the farm.

Next is Porth Oer or Whistling Sands. Turn off, down to car park and then walk. Low cliffs either side of the sand, which whistles if you walk on it when it is dry. It is caused by tiny quartz granules rubbing together.

There are a number of other little coves before you get to Braich y Pwll, the most westerly point. But none of them is an approachable beach.

Much of the gorse and heather clad rough hills belongs to the National Trust and there are footpaths and splendid walking but the seaward side is sheer cliff.

When you drive around, passing Mynydd Anelog, the road takes you down to Aberdaron, passing the holding where Dic Aberdaron lived. Richard Robert Jones, who died in 1845, was completely self-educated and learned at least fourteen languages, wrote a Welsh-Greek-Hebrew dictionary but lost the manuscript, so never had it published. This admirable man loved learning, but there is no evidence that he wished to make himself other than what he was, a vagrant.

Aberdaron's other most prominent son, is Wales's greatest modern poet, Rev. R. S. Thomas, who was vicar until recently.

The last turning before going down into Aberdaron takes you out to Uwchmynydd, a hamlet of sorts, and on to Mynydd Mawr, a dead end, and if you wish to go further, you must walk.

Cliff paths afford splendid walking to the south-west of Aberdaron. Cliffs above the tiny coves of Porth Meudwy, Porth y Pistyll and then

Looking towards Bardsey

Borth. Out of Aberdaron towards Rhiw, on the left, but not visitable as it is private, is Bodwrda, a fine small mansion, altered in Tudor times; and then on the right is Llanfaelrhys Church, alone but well sited a couple of fields from the sea above Porth Ysgo. The church is medieval, long and narrow. Porth Ysgo is National Trust; footpath from the farm leads down to the beach near the waterfall.

The coast between Aberdaron and Rhiw is very pleasant. The two little off-shore islands Ynys Gwylan – fawr and fach (Greater and Lesser Seagull islands) have breeding puffins, among other sea-birds.

Big wedge of National Trust land between Porth Ysgo and Porth Neigwl (Hell's Mouth); very steep, no footpaths seawards but several over the National Trust land leading from Rhiw to Mynydd Rhiw. Here I'm afraid you'll have to rely on the O.S. map 123, 1¼"; it is very good and shows you the interesting things to see.

West side of Porth Neigwl is Mynydd y Craig with Craig Gwineu rising to 800ft., where there is a small fort with stone ramparts, Iron Age before 100A.D. and a number of celtic field patterns. A little further north-east there is a long cairn, but the portal entrance is obstructed by field walls (Tanymuriau); and at Mynydd Rhiw itself is a Stone Axe 'factory', in pits up to 10ft. deep. Not quite like Grime's Graves in East Anglia, but a little industry, nonetheless.

But Rhiw has its own special place and this is Plas yn Rhiw. Lleyn is not a great place for historic houses, there are no Plas Newydds or

Bardsey from Rhiw

Looking towards Yr Eifl

Erddigs, but it is hard to believe that any house in Wales has a better ambiance than this modest little country house. It was given to the National Trust by the Misses Keating in memory of their parents. It stands outside the village overlooking the sea with its gardens going down in terraces. Roses, fuschias, the woods carpeted with snowdrops, an old-fashioned dream world.

The house dates from the first half of the 17th century, but as early as the 10th century Meirion Goch of Rhiw lived here; a descendant, John Lewis, putting his initials and the date 1634 on the rebuilt front. Not a great historic National Trust visiting house, but one which has given intense pleasure in its setting.

Fine walking also at Mynydd Cilan, four miles away, the other end of Porth Neigwl. National Trust as well.

Porth Neigwl or Hell's Mouth is a fine large bay, almost four miles of lonely sand. Difficult off-shore currents and its south-west exposure gave it a fearsome reputation in days of sail. Best access by footpath from Tai Morfa, south-west of Llanengan. Access also from northern end, near Plas yn Rhiw.

The villages of Llandegwning, Llangian and Llanengan merit a mention. Llandegwning is back off the coast road from Porth Neigwl, and its little church is charming. A funny turret and spire, box pews and white painted; inside, a double-decker pulpit. Llangian is a tidy little village of

Llandegwynnin church

the 'best kept' variety. A nice little old chapel, and a church with a unique stone memorial. In the churchyard south of the church is a 5th to 6th century stone inscribed to Melius the doctor, son of Martinus. The use of a profession was not put on memorial stones in Roman times, so this is unique. Also hatchments of the Nanhoron family.

Llanengan is an attractive village; nice pub, Post Office and good church of the 15th century. Re-built over the years, tower added in 1534. Engan or Einion, of Cunedda's line, reputedly buried here, and an offertory chest from a single piece of wood. Double-naved, each with rood-screen. The three bells are believed to have come from St. Mary's Abbey on Bardsey after the Dissolution.

Thence to Abersoch and we are in Holiday-land.

Abersoch has an ideal climate and a superb situation, two splendid beaches bisected by the River Soch. A fine harbour makes it a leading yachting centre; moorings for hundreds of boats. A very popular and in the season crowded centre.

St. Tudwel's Islands are private, preserved as bird sanctuaries. Tugdual, a Breton, founded his cell here in the 6th century and the remains of a much later chapel may be where he founded it on the eastern island; abandoned lighthouse too.

Good walking on the headland between Trwyn Cilan and Trwyn yr Wylfa, Porth Ceiriad in between.

Mynydd Tir y Cwmwd on the seaward side of the main road to Llanbedrog has good walking and fine views. Just inland from the next town Llanbedrog is the scattered village of Mythyno; with wonderful views.

Just off the main road, in fact just about opposite the Warren, with its bungalows and caravans, is, incongruously, Castell March. This 17th century house in its time home to a long line of local notabilities has a strange legend which fits somewhat uneasily with the modern holiday establishments all round.

This was, according to legend, the site of the castle of the King Mark of the Tristan story. And linked with this is the other legend that he had horse's ears and every barber was put to death to keep the secret. But the reeds that came from the place where he buried the bodies, when made into a pipe, would reveal the secret.

Llanbedrog was a village on the hilly road named after Saint Pedrog, a 6th century holy man. Now a newer town has grown up, with lots of holiday homes, though much is obscured in the trees on the hillside. Church, as usual, of several periods: medieval nave with a later chancel; 15th century rood-screen. Nice Victorian chapel too.

Plas Glyn-y-Weddw, a good neo-Gothic mansion, has displays of

Welsh art as well as fine furniture. The then owner of the mansion put a ship's figure-head on the outcrop Tir y Cwm, but this was replaced in 1980 by a modern sculpture called the Tin Man.

The very fine sandy beach down below the village goes right to Pwllheli, good shelter too.

At Penyberth in 1936, the British Government set up an RAF Bombing School and three eminently respectable Welsh Nationalists set fire to it and immediately gave themselves up. A Caernarvon jury refused to convict them so they were taken to London and sentenced to prison there. The original house was knocked down first. There is nothing to see, but this incident was a turning point for modern Welsh nationalism.

Pwllheli, largest town on the peninsula, is a market, and now holiday town. Not much sense of age or history in it, 18th century – a bit – and 19th century buildings, quite a lot and very pleasant, but any sense of shape about the place has been lost. It is ancient, with a charter granted by the Black Prince in 1355. The town was once a considerable port and a good harbour, but silting affected it, but the outer harbour is a fine small boat harbour. Two splendid beaches but be careful of swimming near the Gimblet Rock.

The town has two halves, bisected by the railway: the old town, half a mile inland; and the South Beach and West End, adjoining on the seaward side. The church is Victorian Decorated, and there are a couple of nice chapels especially Penlan and Penmount Methodist Chapel. A good shopping centre by Lleyn standards.

Inland, just off the A497, is Llannor, not improved by its council houses, but it has an inscribed 6th century stone in the church porch. Here we are coming very close to where we started, going through the very rural centre of the peninsula. On the same Nefyn road here is Bodvel Hall (see page 9).

Back to the coast road, Abererch has been a 'best kept' village lots of times – an attractive little place dominated by its church, late medieval alterations and restorations. Named after St. Cawrdaf, 6th century, son of royal family of Brecon. If locked, key probably at the house next door. Opposite is Ebenezer Chapel.

Huge beach of Morfa Aberech goes up to Pen Ychain. This part of the coast is Butlin-land, now entitled Starcoast World, it is a leisure complex, with about every facility imaginable: a Children's Mecca.

On the other side of the road, a single track road leads to Penarth Fawr, a most interesting 15th century manor house. The old timber work is fine and the whole place gives one an unusual idea of a medieval hall house which has not been modernised; 17th century alterations and later

Penarth Fawr

restoration have not harmed the place. Open to visitors, CADW hours. The farm buildings house an interesting craft shop.

Llanystumdwy is an attractive little village, but it is chiefly famous as the home of Lloyd George, whether he is called Earl Lloyd George of Dwyfor or simply David Lloyd George. He was brought up here before going into politics. He represented Caernarvon Boroughs as a Member of Parliament for fifty-five years. He fought hard against Tory landlordism and as well as being the greatest reforming Prime Minister the country has known, he was also remembered by some, such as Hitler, as the man who won the first World War. His boyhood home is opposite The Feathers, his tomb and Museum were designed by Sir Clough Williams-Ellis. Good village walk leaflet.

Cricieth has a pronounced Victorian look, and is all the better for its bay-windowed villas. It has a fine castle; unusually, a Welsh one, not originally built by Edward I, though he did later adapt it. It stands on a rounded hill of hard igneous rock jutting out to sea.

Cricieth Castle

It was not one of the more important castles, but its position is fine. It was strengthened by Edward I (an extra curtain wall and another tower) so it could be held and supplied by sea.

Experts seem to differ as to who did what to it: expertest of all, Sir Charles Oman, seemed to reckon it was all Edwardian, and not by Llewelyn the Great at all. Was the outer ward Welsh? Did Edward I add the two outer towers? Difficult to prove one way or the other; you can be your own expert.

Anyway, very well worth visiting and it is the only castle on the peninsula.

The last word was with Owain Glyndŵr: after he had attacked it in 1401, it was no use to anyone else. But it was, during its time, a royal castle with its royal garrison of about two and a half dozen men.

Sand and shingle beaches on either side of the castle. Houses and cottages round the Green are pleasant and the medieval double-naved church is well restored and worth visiting.

There is another church, St. Deiniol's, which is late Victorian; and a couple of chapels.

The main road A497 goes to Porthmadog but the B4411 leads north through very pleasant countryside, one side road leading to the heart of Snowdonia up to Cwmstradllyn and another, the Dolbenmaen road, to the lovely Pennant valley. Both are fine scenic roads, though both are eventually dead ends.

To the east are the extensive Black Rock sands.

Quite a bit of bungaloid development, but also before reaching Porthmadog there are two little churches, rather neglected in every way. St. Cynhaearn's, Ynyscynhaearn, is on the edge of a marsh, once a lake, Llyn Ystumllyn. It is a mile and a half north-east of Cricieth. Rebuilt in 1820, the fittings are pretty well intact, including a three-decker pulpit – some of the furniture is 17th and 18th century. Treflys is reached by a lane from Pentrefelin off the A497. Originally medieval, much restored last century. There is an uncommon 6th century inscribed pillar stone by the north wall of the nave with a Chi Rho symbol, a monogram made from the two Greek initial letters of Christ.

Before you reach Porthmadog is the village of Borth-y-Gest. It is a seaside village, very pleasant too, with the usual increase of inhabitants into second-home or retirement households. Handy for Porthmadog which it adjoins, decent walking; north-west a couple of miles is the remains of a burial chamber and the hill Moel-y-Gest has good views.

Porthmadog is the southern gateway to the Lleyn peninsula but it is in fact a new town and followed on from the planning and building of Tre-

Borth y Gest

madog. The whole little area here was 'developed' in the early nineteenth century by William Maddocks. He was the son of well-to-do London Welsh parents with roots in north-east Wales. Smitten with the mountainous countryside and the love of wild landscape then fashionable, he moved on to do something useful with it; bought some small farms; built a long embankment and then planned and built a new village called Tremadog. This could have been named after him, or more possibly after the early Welsh prince supposed to have set out from the area to discover America.

There was another motive and that was to improve communications to the north-west in the hope that the route ending at Porth Dinllaen would be chosen as the main point of departure for Ireland. There was, at the turn of the century, contention between Holyhead and Porth Dinllaen. Porth Dinllaen in the event lost by one vote and so Lleyn has remained thankfully unexploited and the A5 and A55 got built where they did, and Holyhead became what it did.

Next step for Maddocks and his invaluable friend and local agent, Williams, was to reclaim the whole vast acreage of Traeth Mawr by the building of what is called The Cob, the embankment which carries the road and the narrow-gauge railway. And then the quarryowners who had had their slates carried by horse-back and loaded out by Ynys Cyngar, west of Borth y Gest, set about creating a harbour, which is now Porthmadog.

And then came the railway. By this time, Maddocks had died. Porthmadog grew haphazardly, attracted coastwise shipbuilding and of course slate exporting. It was never to be a planned town, as Tremadog was, but by the end of Queen Victoria's reign, North Wales slate was roofing the world. But sadly the agricultural improvement of the enclosed Traeth Mawr was, by Maddocks' death, to remain unachieved.

Porthmadog is today hardly an object for architectural admiration; but it is a good shopping centre and although slate is no longer exported, the Ffestiniog narrow-gauge railway is probably more successful than British Rail. Certainly its engines look better.

Some of the somewhat faded and dated elegance of Tremadog can be appreciated even when driving through; though not the fact that Lawrence of Arabia was born there, or the details of the adventures of the 19-year-old Shelley in 1813: he rented Maddocks's house, was attacked and

Penuel, Tremadoc

shot at by a local, ethusiastically tried to help Maddocks by raising money, piled up debts and finally left after the shooting incident.

The road up to Caernarvon opens the way to the Lleyn peninsula on the left and Snowdonia on the right; there is not very much to detain you on a drive between the two towns. On the other hand, the side roads lead to some of the loveliest scenery.

Maps are a bit tricky here: you need 3 1¼" O.S. maps, 115 to cover the top half – you will probably need this anyway, it's the Snowdon area. Then you need the Lleyn map, 123 for the middle part, and finally 124, Dolgellau for the Porthmadog area. Or, as we have said before, Bartholomew's 24 covers the lot, but of course not in such detail, and not footpaths.

The A487 is a good link road between Porthmadog and Caernarvon, in

Small 18th century cottage at Rhostryfan

the summer months probably easier to travel along than the Snowdonia passes. As you travel northwards, any one of the roads on the left will lead you into the peninsula proper which we have tried to describe. For the first half of the journey, about twenty miles in all, the countryside is not spectacular, the land is flattish, rough farming country, with little hills, quiet and by-passed still and the side roads will take you down to Cricieth or Pwllheli. The side roads to the left at Llanllyfni, Penygroes and Croeslon lead to the stunning hill scenery of northern Lleyn.

On the right, there are several real pleasures in store for anyone who does not know the area.

Firstly, the A498 from Tremadog is the main road into Snowdonia and leads to Beddgelert and then on to Snowdonia; or by turning left at Beddgelert up to Caernarvon. The Aberglaslyn Pass before Beddgelert, especially in spring and early summer, is one of the highlights of Welsh scenery; this is where the river came up to before Maddocks built the Cob. Crowded in season; lovely as it is, you may wish you had stuck to Lleyn.

The tiny village of Penmorfa was the edge of the marshy estuary when Maddocks started his reclamation.

Next turn right leads up to Llyn Cwmstradllyn; there is the gaunt ruin of the Ynyspandy Slate Mill, mid-Victorian, something from the past but impressive.

Back on the main road is Bryncir Woollen Mill, a working mill with shop attached and whether you need woollens or not, extremely interesting in its processes.

Following the river Dwyfor is a minor road leading up to Cwm Pennant. This is one part of the Snowdonia area which bears some resemblance to the more remote parts of the Lleyn peninsula. Rough farmland, a little wooded in parts, small hardly viable farms, to the west Moel Hebog and Craig Cwm Silin to the north. The valley comes to a dead end, but you can drive for four or five miles; better even for walking. The Welsh poet Efion Wynn said it better than any description could:

> "Lord, why did you make Cwm Pennant so beautiful,
> and the life of an old shepherd so short."

There was copper mining in Victorian times, and slate quarrying but only ardent industrial archaeologists will want to look for traces; it is rather the half abandoned loneliness that brings most people to this archetype of a half abandoned farming setting.

Dolbenmaen and one or two other semi-villages are met with on the road going north until you come to Llanllyfni; cross the River Llyfni and come to the old quarrying village of Penycroes. Llanllyfni has a pleasant early 19th century interior in Ebenezer chapel; and an unremarkable Iron Age defended post, Caer Engan, a little north-east of the village.

At Penycroes, the road left will take you down to the coast, while that on the right goes via Nantlle to Rhyd-ddu cutting into the Snowdon massif. Nantlle was a substantial slate quarrying area; plenty of evidence. At Croeslon, the Inigo Jones workshop shows the other face of the slate industry, that 'Welshest of Welsh industries', where things are made and finished.

Slate craftmanship of a high standard; and very interesting too. Nearly into Caernarvon, but the proximity and summer bustle of traffic and people should not deter you from going up into the network of tiny roads to the right which bring you to the foothills of Mynydd Mawr via Rhostryfan and Rhosgadfan, the village where Kate Roberts was born a century ago. Some of her novels have been translated and show vividly how hard a life was in the quarrying areas.

Caernarvon (the fort in Arvon) is not nowadays best appreciated on the roads coming in: lots of undistinguished housing and new roads bring one quite suddenly through a short jumble of roads and shopping and there you are, right under the castle walls. This 'magnificent badge of our subjection' as the 18th century traveller Pennant, called it, dominates the town far more than the beautiful castles of Beaumaris and Conwy dominate their towns.

Just outside the town, on the A487, is the Roman fort of Segontium. Like most Roman remains in this country it is little more than a jolly good ground plan, but it and its small museum should be seen, if for nothing more than to get history in perspective. The castle is stupendous and totally intimidating, as it was no doubt intended to be. It can be slightly disappointing at times when you go inside its perfect walls and the number of visitors and absence of interior walls – there is barely a division between wards – gives the impression of a giant garden party.

Do not miss visiting the audio-visual on the installation of the Prince of Wales – a little masterpiece of equivocation which relates the history of the Princes of Wales without giving offence to Welsh or English.

But here is the centre of a system of medieval fortification that is without equal in the world: Caernarvon, Conwy, Beaumaris and Harlech, without mentioning the others. The Edwardian castles, designed and built by the Savoyard, Master James of St. George, are not the subject of this booklet, but anyone getting so near the heart of them, should not fail to visit and study them all.

The town itself had complete walls but unlike Conwy it has not retained them all; much of the town plan is grid patterned and as a town is well worth seeing. It is a very Welsh town. The statue of its M.P. for fifty-five years, Earl Lloyd George, stands in the Castle Square, and it is represented in Westminster today by a Nationalist Member.

Caernarvon Castle

The Beaches of Lleyn

The beaches of Lleyn are excellent, among the best in Wales. While one in three English beaches failed to meet EC standards in 1991, not one on Lleyn failed.

Here is a summary guide, starting at the north.

Fforyd Bay:

It is a large lagoon nearly drying out at low water, at the southern end of the Menai Straits; shallow but unsuitable for swimming – it is mud, shingle and the quicksand as well as the currents make it dangerous. At low tide, it dries into pools and deep channels.

Good for watching waders, oystercatchers, dunlins, curlews, redshank and duck, mallard and teal.

Dinas Dinlle:

The fine, gently shelving beach is three miles long, sweeping north to the Menai Straits. The land behind is low and there is a shingle bank. Parking alongside the beach.

Pontllyfni:

Shingle and rocks, low tide sand, stream on the beach.

Aberdesach:

This is also shingle with a gently shelving beach, both rocks and low tide sand. Parking on the front, access immediate.

Clynnog Fawr:

Long shingly beach with rocks and low water sand. Reached by a path from near the church.

Trefor:

The village has a small shingly and sandy beach. There is another small beach, shingle, to the west beyond the quay. Harbour for small boats.

Porth y Nant:

A shingle beach with low tide sand, steep grassy slopes behind and steep cliffs. Formerly derelict quarry village. Now, Welsh Language Centre.

Pistyll:

A long shingle beach approached by a roadway to the sea; 1 in 4. Parking at the top.

Nefyn:

Splendid stretch of sand almost from Pistyll interrupted by Penrhyn Nefyn headland and continuing on to **Porth Dinllaen** which is another fine stretch terminating in the headland Trwyn Porth Dinllaen which had an Iron Age fort on it.

Penrhyn Cwmister:

Penrhyn Cwmister is of special interest to collectors of shells.

Porth Towyn:

Sandy beach with cliffs behind. Lots of small coves, rock pools.

Porth Ysglaig:

Little headland has inlets either side. Both are sandy; once called the Lonely Beach.

Porth Gwylan:

Sandy beach in a rocky cove, nearly a mile south-west.

Porth Ychen:

Reached by a walk over the headland; tiny cove with shingle and low tide sand.

Traeth Penllech:

Fine long, sandy beach reached by a footpath from the clifftop. Parking is several hundred yards from the beach in a field. Village is Llangwnadl.

Porth Colman:

Not for swimming, but place to park and short walks over cliff to Traeth Penllech.

Porth Iago:

Sandy bay surrounded by rocks, reached by a steep footpath. Strong currents here; swimming can be dangerous.

Porth Oer:

Popular beach backed by steep grassy cliffs, with rocky headlands either side. A steep path from the road, 5 minutes from parking. Sometimes called 'whistling sands', a squeaking noise caused by particles of sand quartz granules which you can make with your feet.

Aberdaron:

A long sandy beach is only one of the village's attractions.

Porth Meudwy, Porth y Pistyll and **Hen Borth** are tiny and reachable by path only – not for swimming.

Port Ysgo:

Sand and shingle beach, but to reach it, 10 minute beside a stream. Once shipped local iron ore.

Porth Cadlan:

Although parking is limited, this is a lovely, relatively little frequented place with a sandy beach and grassy cliffs above the shingle. The coastal scenery is well worth a 10-minute walk through a gorse-clad valley.

Porth Neigwl:

A great wide sandy bay 3½ miles across. It has the English name of Hell's Mouth because of its danger to shipping, and the Welsh name comes from Nigel, who was a follower of the Black Prince.

Porth Bach:

Small shingle beach with low tide sand.

Abersoch:

Wide sandy beach, Porth Fawr going northwards, with sand dunes behind.

Further north, The Warren beach can be reached on foot at low water. South of the village, Porth Bach, a sandy beach. Large caravan site, high dunes and 2 miles of sands.

Llanbedrog:

A popular resort with a beach; steep shingle before flat sand, holiday homes sheltered by the wooded headland, the village exposed.

Pwllheli:

Seaside resort, traditionally chief town of Lleyn; a market town and architecturally satisfying. There is an old town, and a newer suburban part. Inner harbour is silted up but the outer harbour has sailing boats. Beaches: South beach backed by a steep shingle bank is a long sandy beach with dunes behind, extending to Pen y Chain (with Butlins behind it). Safe here.

After Pen y Chain is **Aberwen**, a small beach reached under railway line. Shingle and sand. Small car park, short walk to beach.

Cricieth:

Medieval town of character with a Victorian section grafted on. There are two beaches: that to the east has shingly sand at high tide and sand at low tide. There is a jetty forming a small harbour, and a lifeboat house. The west beach has shingle and sand. There is a long curving Promenade. The town was a centre for the early Welsh princes. Its castle has had a stormy history, taken by Edward I and sacked by Owain Glyndŵr.

The coming of the railway made the town into a pleasant small resort.

Llanystumdwy, close by, was the early home of the great Welsh Prime Minister, Lloyd George; memorial and museum.

There are a couple of footpaths to the beach before Cricieth, but no parking on the main road.

Black Rock Sands (Craig Ddu):

The big sandy beach can be reached along the shore from Cricieth or by road from Morfa Bychan.

There are currents at the south-east end; caves at the Cricieth end under the headland of the rock. Cafe and amenities.

Borth y Gest:

A pleasant bay of shingle and sand, some mud. The estuary has strongish currents. Going south by footpath over the headlands, sandy coves. Footpaths north of the village lead to Moel y Gest, a fine climb of 860ft. Splendid views of the mountains from the top, where there is an Iron Age fort.

Portmadog:

Portmadog was founded by William Maddocks M.P. in the early 19th century. He built the embankment, now called the Cob, across the Glaslyn estuary. It reclaimed some 10,000 acres of farmland and carries road and railway. The name incidentally did not necessarily come from

Maddocks's own name but possibly from the hero of legend, the Prince Madog, who discovered America.

Lloyd George practised as a solicitor in the High Street in Portmadog.

The miniature Festiniog Railway was built originally for carrying slate down from the Ffestiniog quarries to Porthmadog Harbour in 1836.

Portmeirion:

The eminent architect Sir Clough Williams-Ellis emulated William Maddocks in creating his own village. It is an Italianate town, completely artificial, and shows that 'development' does not have to be dull and flat or downright awful. Alas, our planners are rarely of the calibre of Williams-Ellis. There are superb gardens too. You have to pay for a daily visit. The visitors' toll is changed according to season. It is raised only to keep numbers within bounds. If you stay, you don't pay to visit.

Harlech:

A small town with another magnificent castle and a fine beach.

The castle was built by Edward I in 1283 on a high rock by the edge of Morfa Harlech, the Marsh, which stretches up towards Porthmadog. The town was famous in Welsh history even before Edward I for here was the setting of a celebrated story in the early Mabinogion folk-tales.

The beach is half a mile from the town – you walk through dunes N.W. or over the golf links to the south.

Splendid great dunes and long gorgeous sands, but be careful because of currents.

Antiquities

Prehistoric

From early times, there are relics of mankind even in so small an area as Lleyn.

Leaving aside the axes, arrow-heads and other bits and pieces which are in museums, there are some Neolithic burial chambers, remains of the earliest agriculturalists. These date from about 3000 B.C. What one sees are groups of huge stones (megaliths) which were communal burial chambers and covered with turf or stones.

Here are some interesting ones: Bach Wen near Clynnog (Grid Ref. 407495). North of Llanystumdwy, Rhoslan (483409) and Coetan Arthur (498413); near Y Ffor (399384), Cefn Amlwch (230345), and Tan y Muriau by Rhiw (238288).

There was also an extremely unusual archaeological site at Mynydd Rhiw, a prehistoric axe factory (234299).

The Bronze Age, from about 2000 to 800 B.C. has little to show: burials were individual by then, leaving small cairns or tumuli, very often in pretty remote places or hill-tops.

But in the Iron Age 800 to 400 A.D. there are some splendid sites, including one of the best in the country, Tre'r Ceiri on Yr Eifl. Others are Garn Fadryn, Garn Boduan, Garn Pentyrch and Castell Odo.

Roman

There are no good Roman sites nearer than Segontium at Caernarvon where the site Museum is excellent.

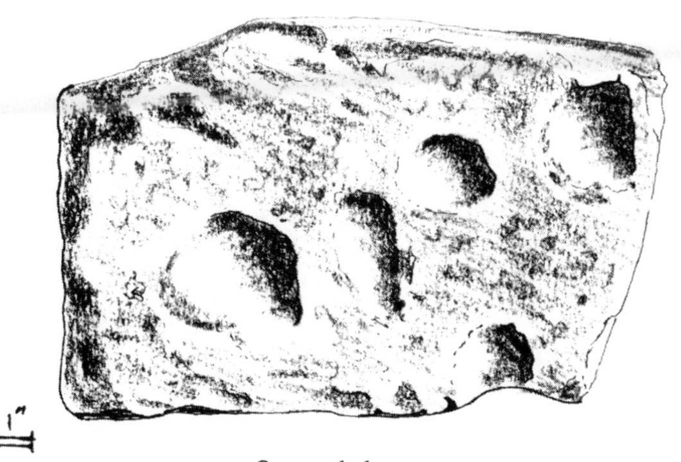

Cup-marked stone

Unique medieval sun-dial at Clynnog

Saints and Churches

Sites from the Age of Saints, or Dark Ages as it is called in England, are the early churches themselves. Most are mentioned in the text: here are the best (although this a matter of opinion really), though all have been restored or rebuilt: Clynnog Fawr, by all accounts the best; Aberdaron, Llanengan, Llangian, Llanbedrog, Llandegwnning, Llanfaelrhys, Rhiw, Bottwnnog, Llaniestyn, Pistyll, Llangwnaddl, Llanfaglan, Treflys, in fact most village churches repay a visit.

Castles

In Lleyn, there is only one castle, Cricieth, which is earlier than the famous Edwardian castles, though it was enlarged by King Edward I. But the finest grouping of defensive castles in the world is within reach, Caernarvon, Conwy, Beaumaris and Harlech; as well as two Welsh castles, Dolbadarn and Dolwyddelan, both in Snowdonia.

Wells

There are holy wells at Clynnog, Llangybi, on the shore below Mynydd Mawr past Aberdaron and Ffynnon Arian at Mynytho. Though these have been 'Christianised', they were probably pagan wells before, with curative powers.

Houses

There are few stately homes in the usual sense, but Plas yn Rhiw (National Trust) and Penarth Fawr near Pwllheli are well worth seeing and so is Llanystumdwy, boyhood home of the great Liberal Prime Minister, Lloyd George.

Irish gold lunula found in a peat-bog near Llanllyfni

What to do in fine weather on Lleyn

First, there are the obvious things ... try the beaches of which there is a good selection on pages 38-42.

Then, just drive in a leisurely way to enjoy the countryside, as we suggest between pages 6 and 37.

You can do it inland, or around the coast. In summer, the latter will always be more crowded.

Try following the Pilgrims' way; this keeps you to the north coast, visiting the churches mentioned in the booklet. But go one better and visit as many as you can of the village churches. There is nothing like them to give you a sense of the history of the area. Try finding the ancient inscriptions.

Try visiting the antiquities: try first the Neolithic burial chambers; they are about five thousand years old. And there are not so many of them that you get bored or have difficulty in remembering which was which, something that might well happen on Anglesey.

Most rewarding, if you are in reasonably good condition, is to visit the Iron Age hill forts, or defended settlements. Tre'r Ceiri is the prize, but there are also Garn Boduan and Garn Fadryn for example. If you get the O.S. Map you'll see them clearly marked, more easily identifiable than on our map.

Bird-watching: if you're an expert, there are a couple of places which you will be making for. Fforyd Bay is good for waders, the cliffs round the Aberdaron end of Lleyn for sea-birds; above all, Bardsey, though whether you will be able to get to the last depends on whether there are any trips; normally one spends a week there.

At Fforyd Bay, if you come from Caernarvon, there is a car park and picnic site past Llanfaglan church. The commoner waders, wildfowl, especially in winter – widgeon, teal, shelduck, oystercatcher, redshank and curlews. But the intertidal sand dune system should be good anytime.

Bardsey is a National Nature Reserve. No unauthorised landings, boatman goes from Aberdaron, ask at Tourist Information Centres for details. It's a splendid place for birds, especially migrants. And choughs too.

Horse-riding near Llanystumdwy and Abersoch, Waunfawr and Llanbedrog.

Castles: on Lleyn there is only Cricieth; best to keep this for a fine day, there is not too much under cover, though you could combine it with shopping in Cricieth, and a visit to Penarth Fawr, or Butlins, or Pwllheli again for shopping.

Golfers will no doubt find the clubs at Porthmadog, Abersoch, Pwllheli, Cricieth and Nefyn.

Tourist Information Centres:

Pwllheli, Y Maes: 075861 3000 (not winter)
Porthmadog, High Street: 0766 512981
Cricieth, 47 High Street: 0766 523303 (not winter)
Conway Castle: 0492 592248
Caernarvon, Oriel Pendeitach: 0286 672232

What to do in dull weather on Lleyn

There is not so much to do on Lleyn as in the rest of Snowdonia. But in fact, the weather is rather better on Lleyn; as in most of Wales the coastal belt is drier and it's only when you come to the mountains, that you get more rain.

When you are not seeing the countryside or on the beaches, see the towns; that won't take long, even if you include Cricieth Castle with the town.

Butlins may attract you, it certainly will the children; it has just about everything. Penarth Fawr and its craft shop is nearby: both to Butlins and Pwllheli. Plas yn Rhiw is a must but you need reasonable weather for the gardens.

There is the Lloyd George Museum at Llanystumdwy and his house, and lovely walks too.

Candle-making and T-shirt printing for the children. There are various attractions in Porthmadog: Maritime museum, craft shops, railways, pottery; and the journey up the road towards Caernarvon then offers Bryncir Woollen Mill and Inigo Jones the slate workshops, both of which are very interesting. You either then go on up to Caernarvon or turn right to Nantlle and on into Snowdonia.

But there are other things to do on Lleyn: Parc Glynllifon to start with. It's on the coast road out of Caernarvon. It has various projects to offer, rather more outdoors than in though.

Most interesting on this coast and in splendid country is the Welsh Country Life Museum at Tai'n Lon near Clynnog; where you can also see the best church in north Wales.

There's a craft shop and farm museum at Tyn Llan, Penmorfa, near Porthmadog.

Bodvel Hall near Pwllheli was where Mrs Thrale, the friend of Dr. Johnson, was born, but more people will be interested in the Adventure Park there now: all sorts of things, both for adults and children. Plas Glyn y Weddw in Llanbedrog is a splendid gothic Victorian mansion with an art gallery. More paintings: Simon van de Put near Pwllheli and Neil Hopkins at Abersoch.

Hand-made furniture at Sarn Mellteyrn, pottery at Trefor, near Yr Eifl.

There seems to have been a diminution of rural craftsmen; there are still potters, artists and other crafts; it is to be hoped that more will set up, especially young local craftsmen. Ask at Tourist Information Centres.

What to see in fine weather further afield

If you take the whole of the Snowdonia National Park as a target, most of north Wales is open to you. But if you are living in the Lleyn area, the further reaches of the National Park give you little time for enjoyment by the time you get there.

And, in summer, can be extremely crowded; it can sometimes be next to impossible to keep one's eyes on the road and to look around.

But if you don't know the Snowdonia area, you must get to it. It is the most beautifully compact mountainous part of Britain. When the National Parks were started, Planning Authorities were faced with the impossible task of keeping the areas concerned wild and beautiful and encouraging the public to come and enjoy them at the same time. It has meant an enormous increase in motor traffic, both private cars and coaches. The National Park Authority have done a valiant job, but when you are faced with summer traffic, it is hard to say, alas, that they have won.

So, the answer is not to drive around more or less aimlessly, but to make for specific destinations. The improved roads from Conway to Caernarvon should now make it possible to avoid traffic jams in the north, but you certainly won't feel you are in the countryside.

If you want to find more beaches, go over to Anglesey or stay on Lleyn.

There are some really fine Nature Reserves, both for bird-watching and Natural History; the Information Centres should give you fuller details.

Bodnant Gardens, National Trust, ten minutes from Conwy on the road to Llanrwst. Plas Newydd at Llanfair pg. on Anglesey, also National Trust, and the most interesting house on view has lovely gardens, ancient monuments and a situation on the Menai Straits.

One unique activity in north Wales is getting around on the narrow-gauge railways. There are more and better than anywhere else in Britain, and they show you finer scenery. It is arguable, but possibly the finest scenery is that seen from Ffestiniog Railway which goes from Porthmadog up to Blaenau Ffestiniog. It's an hour journey each way, you need fine weather, and it's not cheap, but it is good value. There are others, perhaps more suitable at times – depends what you are looking for: there's a useful leaflet on the Great Little Trains. In total, there are the Snowdon Mountain Railway at Llanberis, Llanberis Lake, Bala Lake, Welsh Highland (Porthmadog) and Tal-y-Llyn. They all offer a different length of ride and go over various terrains, but all good.

What to do in dull weather further afield

A few years ago, a wet day in the summer months would mean enormous lines of cars to clog up the roads, since nobody was on the beaches and you couldn't see above 200 feet or so. Nowadays, it's much better. There are plenty of theme parks and indoor things to do. And, the Information Offices have a splendid amount of stuff available.

First places to make for if you want to find more than one thing to see or do are the towns of Caernarvon, Conwy and Beaumaris. You will have to accept lots of people though. But the castles built for King Edward I by Master James of St. George are probably the finest grouping of castles in the world. There are four in north Wales, the three mentioned in the towns bearing their names and Harlech, where the town is much smaller. The other Edwardian castles are outside our area and are possibly less interesting anyway. They were all built to ensure that Wales never became an independent country again: 'the magnificent badge of our subjection' as Pennant called Caernarvon, which is certainly the most imposing. Plenty of literature in the castles themselves and very good it is, especially the little exhibition boards which seem to be all the rage these days. They are managed by Welsh Historic Monuments (CADW).

There are other castles: Dolbadarn and Dolwyddelan, both CADW, Penrhyn which is National Trust, Bryn Bras and Gwydir which are private. Don't bother about Dolbadarn or Dolwyddelan in bad weather, and no CADW places have refreshments, though the main ones are in towns. Further afield is Bodelwyddan in Clwyd. To choose one place against another is hard, but Conwy is best in some ways because of the other houses you can visit: Aberconway House, the medieval National Trust house; Plas Mawr: a magnificent Elizabethan town house, one of the finest in Britain, and then in a different category, the 'smallest house in Britain' down on the quay. And then Telford's bridge and Stephenson's railway bridge, and the medieval town walls, the best in Britain. And if the weather turns out fine, Bodnant Gardens only ten minutes away up the Conwy valley. In Rhyl there's the Sun Centre and the Knight's Cavern for starters and the Welsh Mountain Zoo at Colwyn Bay.

The slate industry is worth a good half day: Blaenau Ffestiniog has Llechwedd and Glodfa Ganol, is unique, with Llanberis as an alternative and yet another slate museum at Llanfair, near Harlech. Inigo Jones at Croeslon on the Caernarvon-Porthmadog road really does show how slate can be attractively used nowadays.

Woollen mills at Bryncir just north of Tremadog, Trefriw in the Conwy valley, Penmachno near Betws y Coed, both to watch an up-to-date version of an old craft and the opportunity to buy high quality Welsh woollens.

The other towns of north Wales which are reasonably accessible should not be omitted; they all have a distinctive personality. Llandudno is the most perfect Victorian holiday resort in Britain and the Great Orme has a list of attractions: Country Park, Summit Complex, fascinating history and archaeology. Caernarvon, an up-dated medieval town, quite apart from its castle which, despite holiday crowds, it would be very remiss not to see. In any case, you should not miss the audio-visual of the history of the Princes of Wales, which manages to give the history of the English rape of Wales without giving offence to either English or Welsh. Segontium Roman site and museum is on the A485 just out of Caernarvon; and the Air Museum and airport is out of the town on the Lleyn side.

Anglesey

Beaumaris too is well worth a visit – fine weather as well as wet – for its castle, both aesthetically beautiful and the culmination of the techniques of castle building. The court-house opposite the castle, and the jail, if you feel masochistic enough.

If you are over on Anglesey, for visiting Beaumaris, go on past the town to the lovely little complex of buildings at Penmon. The ancient monuments of Anglesey, especially the earliest, are quite well worth a whole day. There's an indispensable CADW booklet, and a day's wandering through unspoilt countryside reveals some quite astonishing aspects of life around four thousand years ago. Actually this is better done when it's fine, or at least not pouring.

In the other direction from Beaumaris, there is Llanfair pg. If you want to be photographed by that railway sign which is really only a linking of two village names, Llanfairpwllgwyngyllgogerwchwrndrobwllllantisiliogogogoch (you can visit both churches), and do some shopping in Pringle's giant shop.

But just down the road is Plas Newydd (National Trust) and its fine gardens, possibly the best private house to visit; and a little further on again, the Anglesey Sea Zoo (under cover), Bird World, the Nature Reserve of Newborough Warren and so on.

Before this little outline get out of hand, pay a visit to one of the Tourist Information Centres and get some of the leaflets about other places to visit.

Here are some of a widely varying selection:

Central Snowdonia

Sygun Copper Mine near Beddgelert: Mining was one of the oldest activities of Snowdonia, and central Wales too. This is one of very few to give one an idea of what it was all about. Parys Mountain, in Anglesey, was the grat copper mine; open-cast scars are still there. Most copper mines have just disappeared.

Slate quarrying we have already mentioned, but that was up at

Blaenau Ffestiniog. At Llanberis there is the enormous former Dinorwic complex – in fact the Llanberis area could occupy a couple of days. There's Padarn Country Park, and across the road, the Snowdon Mountain Railway.

There is a turning off the A487 to the seaward side between Porthmadog and Penrhyndeudraeth and down a narrow wooded road is one of the most attractive places in Britain. Fine in dull weather, but at its best on sunny days to see the gardens too.

This is Portmeirion, an example of total development, starting from scratch and becoming a village. It was built by Sir Clough Williams-Ellis throughout the twenties and it is a work of art that can be unreservedly enjoyed for its eccentricities as well as anything else. It's better when you stay there since the crowds melt away after five o'clock. (There is a charge during the day to limit the crowds.) The hotel down by the waterfront has some fine exaggerated Indian decor, there are lots of furnished apartments in the village and book, pottery, antique shops sort of thing. Miles of fine walking and an abundance of sand; and splendid gardens

Whether or not Portofino or some other Italian village provided inspiration is beside the point; Sir Clough used all sorts of fine old buildings and architectural bits and pieces, as well as visual tricks to create something unique. It was a bit elitist before the war, but the crowds now show that everyone (and it's sometimes like that despite the entry charge) can enjoy it. Pick good weather though. If you are interested get Williams-Ellis's own books on it and his work as a conservationalist is fit to stand beside Ruskin and William Morris. If you are old enough for it to mean anything, Noel Coward wrote 'Blithe Spirit' and 'The Prisoner' series was made here.

It won't take long to get further south: go down the coast road to Harlech, though the traffic can be heavy. But it leads you to the Mawddach Estuary. Dolgellau is just about at the edge of the National Park. But Dolgellau and Machynlleth are pleasant to visit and the scenery beyond and going inland is wild and lovely.

Shell Island (Mochras), Maes Artro and Corris – getting far from Snowdonia by car – are well worth a visit on a good day as well as bad.

If you go south towards Dolgellau on the fast A470 instead of by Harlech, go up to the Visitor Centre at Coed-y-Brenin and find out something about the importance and extent of forests in Snowdonia.

Best thing is to visit a Tourist Information Centre and work through the leaflets.

Notes on Folk Tales and Legends

In Victorian times, a belief in fairies was general. They were called the Fair People, 'Y Tylwyth Teg'. Stories about them play such a dominant part in Welsh folk-lore that they seem almost a parallel population of the country.

In some areas, they were small and rather unpleasant, went to fairs, stole from farmers and played unkind tricks; stole butter and cheese, milked the cows and goats, carried away unbaptised infants, replacing them with their own peevish babies but sometimes they were bigger and stronger and better dressed, more elegant, and rewarded humans who were good to them.

Another species was beautiful and honest. They were a sort of upper class fairy, spending a lot of time dancing in the moonlight, and riding their small grey horses. They would come to farmhouses at night and leave money for any milk or bread they took. An Abersoch woman lent them a griddle to bake white bread. They often borrowed farm or kitchen tools, and left money to pay. They liked to find things neat and clean. Sometimes on Lleyn and in the area of Yr Eifl, shepherds would meet them and talk. There are endless tales of meetings and marriages with Tylwyth ladies. A prototype of such tales goes like this.

One moonlight night, the son of Ystrad Farm went to Lake Cwellyn in the Nant y Betws area and hid, to watch the Tylwyth Teg dancing. He saw a beautiful girl whom he fell in love with.

On a sudden impulse, he leaped into the ring, seized the girl and made off with her. He got her home and treated her so well that she agreed to be a farm servant. She did her work wonderfully well especially the milking; the cows seemed to give twice as much for her. One thing she would not do, and that was to give her name.

Then quite accidentally one night driving a couple of cows to their grazing, the young man came to the place he had captured the fairy girl. He hid and overheard two fairies saying: "When we were last here, our sister Penelope was stolen by a man." He went home and called her by her name, which greatly surprised and upset her.

He asked her to marry him; at first she wouldn't, but later agreed with one condition: that he should never strike her with iron. If he did, she would leave him for ever. He readily agreed and they lived happily for many years. They had a family and prospered. Then one day, they went out to a field to catch a horse which was untamed and while they were at work, he rashly threw the bridle over the horse while the wife was close by, and the iron touched her. She immediately disappeared and was never heard from again – except on one cold wintry night when she came to his bedroom window and told him to take care of the children.

This tale might be called the prototype of many legends, especially in north Wales, of human-fairy marriages. Nearly all follow the same pattern except that the hiding of a fairy's name is an element of the international folk-tale that has somehow found its way in.

Mixed marriages and cases of men being absorbed into Tylwyth dances are most common. In the event of the latter, it needed a strong man and a length of mountain ash, to pull a man out. Fairies withheld their names and a number of tales are concerned with finding out.

A farmer's wife who lived at the nant in Llaniestin parish was frequently visited by a fairy who used to borrow her 'padell a gradell' (used in cooking bread) and repay her with a loaf, carried on her head. One day the fairy came to borrow her wheel for spinning flax. When she handed it over, the farmer's wife asked the fairy's name as she came so often, but the fairy refused to tell her. But as she watched her spinning, the fairy sang to the whirl of the wheel:

Bychan a wydda' hi	Little did she know
Mai Sili go Dwt	That Sili go Dwt
Yw f'enw i	Is my name.

A Corwrion fairy sang much the same ditty when she came out of the water to spin.

Sili Ffrit or Dwt was often said to be the name of a girl descended from a fairy family.

There are plenty of other tales, and here are a few.

A man fell in love with a beautiful Tylwyth lady and wanted to marry her. She consented but warned him that she would leave him if he ever touched her with iron. He accepted the condition but thought little of it. They were married and lived happily for many years and had several children. But an accident happened to them one day. They were crossing Traethmawr at Penrhyndeudraeth on horseback together when the man's horse became restive and jerked his head towards the wife and the bit of the bridle by accident touched her left arm. She told her husband that she must leave him straight away. He was terribly upset and implored her not to. She said she could not stay.

Then he appealed to her love for the children and begged that she would stay for them. What, he said, would happen to them without their mother.

Her strange answer was: "Let them be redheaded and longnosed."

Then she disappeared and was never seen again. But there was in fact a type of Welshman with these characteristics, redhaired and longnosed. The Wild Men of Mawddwy were like this. The Wild Red Men began their outlawry in the 11th century, but Tacitus mentions redhaired Britons, so it is difficult to date their first appearance.

Many of the Tylwyth were thought to live in caves beneath Mount Eilio and several tales of men meeting beautiful Tylwyth girls and marrying them came from this area. The marriage was invariably successful, the wives being particularly good at handling stock, but they were never to be touched by iron, or they would leave their husbands and children, though they sometimes maintained contact with the latter.

The mixed marriages and the prohibition of being touched by iron may well be a culture conflict going back to the coming of the Celtic (Iron Age) people and their relationship with the earlier, Bronze Age, people.

The better-off ones used to hire a human midwife from time to time. But this was a risky business.

An interesting tale of a midwife was told by Pali Evans who died a hundred years ago. She had been called to attend a Tylwyth confinement and found everything in splendid order for it was a very grand house and the lady was the wife of one of the princes. But Pali could see nothing but the lady and the baby. Everything was done noiselessly and Pali saw nobody else. She was given ointment to rub the baby with after bathing it morning and night, and she was warned not to put any near her eyes. One day her eye happened to itch and she rubbed it; she saw everything much more clearly. Small men and women were going quietly about, preparing food and looking after the lady carefully, the house and furniture were luxurious. Pali said to her, "You have had a great many visitors today." "How do you know," said the lady. "You have put the ointment into your eyes." And straightaway she got out of bed and blew into Pali's eyes, and said, "Now you will see no more." From then on, she never saw the fairies again. Nor was the ointment entrusted to her again. According to a slightly similar version, the midwife went to Ffair Rhos between Ystrad Meurig and Pontrhydfendigaid. There she saw a great many of the Tylwyth including the lady she had attended. When she went up and greeted her, the lady spat in her face, and she never managed to see the fairies again.

There were mermaids too. Here is a classic Nefyn mermaid tale which is told in other areas too.

One fine September afternoon at the beginning of the eighteenth century, a fisherman named Pergrin, was fishing. Thinking he saw some movement, he went silently inshore towards a recess in the cliffs, and there on a rock, he saw a mermaid combing her hair. Quietly but carefully he came alongside and, jumping out, seized her and carried her back on board, struggling wildly and threshing about with her tail. But Pergrin had got her securely and she could not get away.

We do not know what language mermaids speak normally, but this one spoke fluent Welsh and between her tears she begged Pergrin to let her go. But it is not every day that one finds a mermaid and he was most reluctant, although he was rather distressed to see how upset she was. Then, with a last effort, she said, "Pergrin, if you will let me go, I will give three shouts to you in your hour of greatest need." So Pergrin released her, thinking he would never really see her again. And for weeks he did not. Then one hot afternoon, when the sea was calm and Pergrin and a number of other fishermen were out fishing, he suddenly saw the head and shoulders of the mermaid appear in the sea by his boat.

"Pergrin, Pergrin, Pergrin," she cried urgently. "Take up your nets. Take up your nets."

Pergrin was surprised for the afternoon was fine, and the sea showed no sign of any danger. But he instantly pulled in his nets with haste and back he went, past the bar and no sooner was he in than a terrible storm broke out. Eighteen others who had gone out were all drowned.

At Cricieth, two musicians went into Ogo Ddu and their music, pipe and horn, was heard; but they never came out. One was playing Ffarwel Dic y Pibydd and the other Ffarwel Twm Bach, or possibly Ffarwel Ned Puw.

Not too far away at Llangybi, there was a buried treasure story about Garn Pentyrch, on which there had been an Iron Age fort.

There was a stone on top so heavy and fixed so fast that no men or horses could move it. One day a little girl playing there moved it with the touch of her hand and a store of coins was found beneath. Similar tales are found elsewhere, except that at Llyn Ogwen, the belief was that a Gwyddel (an Irishman) would find it. Garn Fadryn had a large flat stone on top, Bwrdd y Brenin, Arthur's Table, also concealing a pot of gold; the stone was also thought to have some connection with the Stone of Destiny at Westminster.

This Aberdaron story has more than a hint of humour and has a faintly Irish air about it:

A farmer living at Deunant near Aberdaron, used to go out of his house a few steps every night to relieve himself before going to bed. But one night while he stood there, a stranger was standing beside him.

"You have no idea," said the stranger, "how annoying this is for me and my family."

"But how can that be?" said the farmer.

"My house is directly below," said the stranger. "Just stand on my foot and you will see what I mean."

The farmer did so, and he could see how all his slops went straight down the other's chimney which stood far below in a road he had never seen before.

The fairy then suggested he had a door made on the other side of the house and that if he did so, his cattle would never suffer from anthrax. The farmer did this and he became the most prosperous stock rearer in the area.

One of Arthur's warriors was March Amheirchion, lord of Castellmarch, near Abersoch, in Lleyn; and he had horse's ears. He kept his hair long and to prevent anyone knowing his secret, he killed every barber who came to shave him and cut his hair.

On the spot where he used to bury the bodies, reeds grew and when these were cut to make a pipe, it played no other sound than: 'March Amheirchion has horse's ears'. When March heard this he would probably have killed the innocent player on the spot, except that even he himself, could not make the pipe play another tune.

So he gave up the pretence and had his hair cut normally.

This tale is interesting in that it dates back to a time when a pipe, not the harp, was the favourite musical instrument. And there was an ancient Irish King with horse's ears. But of course this is the story of King Midas from Greek mythology. Or was this originally an old Celtic story brought with the movement of Celtic-speaking peoples from south-eastern Europe?

There is another class of folk-tale, and these deal with Saints.

In the sixth century, Saintship was already a profession in Wales, especially in the west and north. The Saints were, in many cases, itinerant monks coming from princely families. They sailed round the dangerous and rocky west and north coasts and founded their tiny cells, living simply and preaching their austere gospel, sometimes individually or sometimes in a community.

Nothing was recorded of their activities for hundreds of years, and when their biographies were written, the credulity of medieval religiosity revealed some strange things.

Heads were cut off, picked up and put back. Among others St. Winifred, St. Justinan, St. Cynog and St. Decumen suffered in this way. St. Piran sailed from Ireland on a sea monster, St. Feock on a granite boulder, and St. Decumen, as well as his headless accomplishment, sailed on a bundle of twigs.

St. Brendan, riding from Ireland on a sea monster, met St. Barre riding the opposite way on a horse.

The austere St. David confined his miracles on the whole to occurrences of a religious nature – healing his teacher Paulinus's blindness, or raising a hill at Llandewi Brefi on which to preach against Pelagianism.

At times, saintliness got mixed up with the fairies and their magic world: St. Collen has a successful set-to with Gwyn ap Nudd, King of the Underworld.

Quite a few stories have concerned Beuno.

When St. Beuno lived at Clynnog, he used to preach regularly at Llanddwyn. Walking along the shore one day, he dropped his book of sermons and it was swept away by the tide.

He looked for it everywhere and finally found it again, with a curlew standing beside it keeping guard. Beuno fell to his knees and asked the Lord to bless the curlew and the Lord granted the blessing of making the curlew's nest very hard to find.

Beuno was a formidable man, much given to cursing his opponents, and with some effect. His most well-known exploit was not here in Lleyn, but at Holywell where he helped his niece Gwenfrewi or Winifred.

Caradog, the son of a local chieftain Alyn from Penarleg (Hawerden) 'endeavoured to force her chastity', but, having taken her vows, she resisted, and fled to St. Beuno's church. Beuno had left Berriew on the Welsh border, because he heard an English voice. Caradog chased her and when she still repulsed him, drew his sword and cut off her head. A healing well gushed forth where the head fell. Her head rolled gently down the hill to the church. The congregation, surprised to see the head roll in, went outside to find the murderer wiping his sword 'on the grasse'. Beuno picked up the head and cursed the young man who died on the spot and disappeared from sight. The saint then joined the head to the body, covering it with his mantle, and returned to the church to say Mass, and prayed. The girl rose up 'as if from sleep', with a white circle, as small as a thread, round her neck. She spent the rest of her life as a nun, becoming Abbess at Gwytherin in Denbighshire.

Winifred sent Beuno a cloak, placing it on a stone and the sea took it from Holywell around to Lleyn where Beuno found it, perfectly dry.

St. Aelhaearn, a pupil of Beuno, had the misfortune to be savaged by wild beasts and St. Beuno tended him, but found he was lacking part of his face, so replaced part of his brow with an iron pikestaff. Aelhaearn was called after this event from then on.

Beuno was said to have replaced six heads, according to a short *Life of Beuno,* in Welsh, written in 1346; perhaps St. Beuno's activities became a trifle exaggerated with time.

When he died, Clynnog, Nefyn and Bardsey all wanted his body, and the appearance of three coffins undoubtedly appeased them.

Index

Glossary

aber estuary, confluence
afanc beaver
afon river
allt hill, hillside, slope, wood
ap son of
ar on, upon, over, by

bach, (*adj.*) small, little, lesser
ban peak, crest
banc bank, hill, slope
bangor monastery with a wattle fence
bedwen birch
bedd grave
betws chapel
blaen head, source of river
bod abode
braich spur, arm
bro region, vale, lowland
bryn hill
bwlch pass, gap
bychan little, small, lesser

cadair seat
cae field
caer fort
canol middle
capel chapel, meeting house
carn cairn, rock
carreg stone, rock
castell castle, stronghold
cefn ridge
celli grove, copse
cemais river bends
cennin leek
ceunant ravine, gorge, brook
cil retreat
clawdd dyke, hedge, ditch
clogwyn precipice, crag
clun meadow
cnwc hillock
coch red
coed trees, wood, forest
cors bog
craig rock
crib crest, summit, arête
croes cross, cross-roads
croesffordd, croeslon cross-roads
crug knoll, tump
cwm valley, combe
cwrt court, yard

dan under, below
dau, *f.* **dwy** two
derwen oak
diffwys desolate place
dinas hill fortress
dol meadow
drws gap, narrow pass
du, *f.* **ddu** black, dark

dwfr, dŵr water
dyffryn valley

eglwys church
eithin furze, gorse
esgair ridge

ffin boundary
fforch bifurcation, fork
ffordd way, road
ffos ditch, trench
ffridd rough grazing
ffrwd stream, torrent
ffynnon spring, well

garth enclosure
garw rough, coarse
gefail smithy
glan river-bank, bank, hillock
glas green, blue
glyn deep valley, glen
gwaun mountain pasture
gwern place where alders grow
gwyn, *f.* **gwen** white
gwyrdd green

hafod summer-dwelling
haidd barley
haul the sun
helygen willow
hen old
hendre(f) winter dwelling
heol, hewl road
hir long

is below, under
isaf lower, lowest
isel low

llain narrow strip of land
llan church, enclosure
llannerch clearing, glade
llawr flat valley bottom
llech slab, slate
llechwedd hillside
llety small house, shelter
llethr slope
lluest hut, cottage
llwch lake
llwyd grey, brown
llwyn grove, bush
llyn lake
llys court, hall

maen stone
maes field
mawr great, big
melin mill
melindre(f) mill village
melyn yellow
merthyr burial place, church

moel bare hill, bald
morfa marsh, sea fen
mur wall
mwyn ore, mine
mynachlog monastery
mynydd mountain, moorland

nant brook
newydd new

odyn kiln
onnen ash tree

pandy fulling mill
pant hollow, valley
parc park, field
pen head, top, end
penrhyn promontory
pentre(f) village, homestead
pistyll spout, waterfall
plas hall, mansion
pont bridge
porth gateway, harbour
pwll pit, pool

rhaeadr waterfall
rhiw hill, slope
rhos, *pl.* **rhosydd** moorland
rhyd ford

sain, san, sant, saint saint
sarn causeway
sych dry

tafarn tavern
tal end
tan end, below
teg fair
tir land, territory
tomen mound
ton grassland, lea
traeth strand, beach, shore
trallwng wet bottom land
tre(f) homestead, hamlet, town
tri, *f.* **tair** three
troed foot
tros over
trum ridge
trwyn point, cape
twyn hillock, knoll
tŷ, *pl.* **tai** house
tyddyn, ty'n small farm

uchaf upper, higher, highest
uwch above, over

y, yr, 'r, *(definite article)* the
ych ox
yn in
ynys island
ysbyty hospital, hospice
ystrad valley floor, strath
ystum bend (in river)

Maps

The sketch map in this booklet is adequate in outline. But you do need an O.S. map for finding your way once you get off the main roads. Sadly there isn't one 1¼" which is adequate. Sheet 123 entitled Lleyn cuts off too much in the east and will not get you to Caernarvon or Porthmadog, so it is no good for going over to Snowdonia. Equally, the Snowdonia map is no good for Lleyn, or for the southern part of Snowdonia if it comes to that. So you will need yet another 1¼" O.S. map, Dolgellau O.S. 124 as well. The best single map is Bartholomew number 27, North Wales, except that it cuts Lleyn in half, though it does give it all.

We are following the O.S. practice in the spelling of names, though this may not follow the usage accepted by the University of Wales.